HowExpert

How To Study The Bible For Beginners

Your Step By Step Guide To Studying The Bible

HowExpert with Jane Rodda

Copyright HowExpert™
www.HowExpert.com

For more tips related to this topic, visit HowExpert.com/studybible.

Recommended Resources

- HowExpert.com – Quick 'How To' Guides on All Topics from A to Z by Everyday Experts.
- HowExpert.com/free – Free HowExpert Email Newsletter.
- HowExpert.com/books – HowExpert Books
- HowExpert.com/courses – HowExpert Courses
- HowExpert.com/clothing – HowExpert Clothing
- HowExpert.com/membership – HowExpert Membership Site
- HowExpert.com/affiliates – HowExpert Affiliate Program
- HowExpert.com/writers – Write About Your #1 Passion/Knowledge/Expertise & Become a HowExpert Author.
- HowExpert.com/resources – Additional HowExpert Recommended Resources
- YouTube.com/HowExpert – Subscribe to HowExpert YouTube.
- Instagram.com/HowExpert – Follow HowExpert on Instagram.
- Facebook.com/HowExpert – Follow HowExpert on Facebook.

COPYRIGHT, LEGAL NOTICE AND DISCLAIMER:

COPYRIGHT © BY HOWEXPERT™ (OWNED BY HOT METHODS). ALL RIGHTS RESERVED WORLDWIDE. NO PART OF THIS PUBLICATION MAY BE REPRODUCED IN ANY FORM OR BY ANY MEANS, INCLUDING SCANNING, PHOTOCOPYING, OR OTHERWISE WITHOUT PRIOR WRITTEN PERMISSION OF THE COPYRIGHT HOLDER.

DISCLAIMER AND TERMS OF USE: PLEASE NOTE THAT MUCH OF THIS PUBLICATION IS BASED ON PERSONAL EXPERIENCE AND ANECDOTAL EVIDENCE. ALTHOUGH THE AUTHOR AND PUBLISHER HAVE MADE EVERY REASONABLE ATTEMPT TO ACHIEVE COMPLETE ACCURACY OF THE CONTENT IN THIS GUIDE, THEY ASSUME NO RESPONSIBILITY FOR ERRORS OR OMISSIONS. ALSO, YOU SHOULD USE THIS INFORMATION AS YOU SEE FIT, AND AT YOUR OWN RISK. YOUR PARTICULAR SITUATION MAY NOT BE EXACTLY SUITED TO THE EXAMPLES ILLUSTRATED HERE; IN FACT, IT'S LIKELY THAT THEY WON'T BE THE SAME, AND YOU SHOULD ADJUST YOUR USE OF THE INFORMATION AND RECOMMENDATIONS ACCORDINGLY.

THE AUTHOR AND PUBLISHER DO NOT WARRANT THE PERFORMANCE, EFFECTIVENESS OR APPLICABILITY OF ANY SITES LISTED OR LINKED TO IN THIS BOOK. ALL LINKS ARE FOR INFORMATION PURPOSES ONLY AND ARE NOT WARRANTED FOR CONTENT, ACCURACY OR ANY OTHER IMPLIED OR EXPLICIT PURPOSE.

ANY TRADEMARKS, SERVICE MARKS, PRODUCT NAMES OR NAMED FEATURES ARE ASSUMED TO BE THE PROPERTY OF THEIR RESPECTIVE OWNERS, AND ARE USED ONLY FOR REFERENCE. THERE IS NO IMPLIED ENDORSEMENT IF WE USE ONE OF THESE TERMS.

NO PART OF THIS BOOK MAY BE REPRODUCED, STORED IN A RETRIEVAL SYSTEM, OR TRANSMITTED BY ANY OTHER MEANS: ELECTRONIC, MECHANICAL, PHOTOCOPYING, RECORDING, OR OTHERWISE, WITHOUT THE PRIOR WRITTEN PERMISSION OF THE AUTHOR.

ANY VIOLATION BY STEALING THIS BOOK OR DOWNLOADING OR SHARING IT ILLEGALLY WILL BE PROSECUTED BY LAWYERS TO THE FULLEST EXTENT. THIS PUBLICATION IS PROTECTED UNDER THE US COPYRIGHT ACT OF 1976 AND ALL OTHER APPLICABLE INTERNATIONAL, FEDERAL, STATE AND LOCAL LAWS AND ALL RIGHTS ARE RESERVED, INCLUDING RESALE RIGHTS: YOU ARE NOT ALLOWED TO GIVE OR SELL THIS GUIDE TO ANYONE ELSE.

THIS PUBLICATION IS DESIGNED TO PROVIDE ACCURATE AND AUTHORITATIVE INFORMATION WITH REGARD TO THE SUBJECT MATTER COVERED. IT IS SOLD WITH THE UNDERSTANDING THAT THE AUTHORS AND PUBLISHERS ARE NOT ENGAGED IN RENDERING LEGAL, FINANCIAL, OR OTHER PROFESSIONAL ADVICE. LAWS AND PRACTICES OFTEN VARY FROM STATE TO STATE AND IF LEGAL OR OTHER EXPERT ASSISTANCE IS REQUIRED, THE SERVICES OF A PROFESSIONAL SHOULD BE SOUGHT. THE AUTHORS AND PUBLISHER SPECIFICALLY DISCLAIM ANY LIABILITY THAT IS INCURRED FROM THE USE OR APPLICATION OF THE CONTENTS OF THIS BOOK.
**COPYRIGHT BY HOWEXPERT™ (OWNED BY HOT METHODS)
ALL RIGHTS RESERVED WORLDWIDE.**

Table of Contents

Recommended Resources 2
Introduction 6
    Studying the Bible 6
    What Difference Does It Make? 7
    How the Guide is Laid Out 8
Chapter 1: Before You Start 11
    Things to Do 11
    Remember This 12
    And Don't Forget This..13
Chapter 2: Prayer..14
    Why Prayer Matters 14
    Step-By-Step Guide to Prayer 15
    What to Do 16
    What Not To Do 17
Chapter 3: Choose the Bible You Want to Use......................19
    Why there are So Many Bibles 19
    Some of the Different Translations 19
    Types of Bibles 20
    Which Bible Is Best For You? 21
Chapter 4: Choose the Book You Want to Study 22
    Why Choosing the Book Matters 22
    Step-By-Step Guide to Choosing the Book 24
    What to Do 25
    What Not To Do 25
    Overview of the Books of the Bible 26
    Old Testament 26
Chapter 5: What to Read When 37

What to Read When You are Feeling 37
What to Read When You are Sad 38
What to Read When You are Angry 39
What to Read When You are Happy 40
What to Read When You Feel Like Giving Up 41
What to Read When You are Sick 43
What to Read When You are Lonely 44
What to Read during this Major Life Event... 46
What to Read When You are Starting College 47
What to Read When You are Falling in Love 49
What to Read When You are Getting Married 51
What to Read When You are Having Children 52
What to Read When You Have Lost a Loved One 54

Chapter 6: Move From the Outside In 57
Step-By-Step 57

Chapter 7: Apply It To Your Life 60
What to Do 60
What Not To Do 61

Chapter 8: Seek Wise Counsel 63
Find a Church 63
Step-By-Step Guide to Finding a Church 64
Find a Mentor 66
Find Fellowship 66
Ways to Find Fellowship 67

Chapter 9: Conclusion 70
Bibliography 71
About the Expert 72
Recommended Resources 73

Introduction

Studying the Bible

Why do we study the Bible? This is an important question to ask, and an important question to answer. There are several long, philosophical answers that have been given, and there are people who have spent their entire lives devoted to answering that very question. I could try to go on and on with arguments in an attempt to prove why we should devote our time to studying the Bible, but to me the answer is simple. We study the Bible because it's God's Word.

There are a million different things in this world demanding our time. There are false teachers who want to distract us. There are temptations around every corner. There is anger and sadness and despair. If you try and combat all of this on your own, you will fail. It's as simple as that. But if you spend time reading and studying God's word and letting it transform your life, it makes it easier to face the challenges of living in a sinful world.

Notice that I said easier – not easy. I don't want you to be misled into the belief that if you devote your time to studying the Bible then suddenly your life will be simple and problem free. You will still have trials and temptations, and still face the same issues you faced before you began looking to the Word. But you will be armed. You will have knowledge of the scriptures, and you will be able to rely on the hope and promise of God.

Hebrews 4:12 says, "The word of God is living and powerful, and sharper than any two-edged sword, piercing even to the division of soul and spirit, and of joints and marrow, and is a discerner of the thoughts and intents of the heart." If you go to God's word with the expectation that it should and will change your life, you will not be disappointed.

What Difference Does It Make?

The difference that it makes can be summed up with two words: peace and hope. I know this sounds trite, but it is the truest statement I can think of. When you study the Bible, you will be able to view situations differently. You will be able to cling to God's promises. You will know that there is more to life than our own thoughts and limitations, and you will know that the sufferings of today will not last forever.

I have had an amazing example of this happen in my own life over the past few months, even as I have been writing this guide. I am a mom to four children, three of whom play baseball. My husband also works as a coach for a middle school baseball team, and he and I coach our daughter's team. So basically the last two months have been nothing but baseball. I made up a color-coded calendar to help keep all of the practices and games straight, and when it was finished I looked at it and laughed. It wasn't necessarily a happy laugh, but more a laugh of, "How in the world are we going to do all of this?" Other than Sundays, every single day of the week had something scheduled, whether a game or a practice, and usually at least two activities. I had no idea how we were going to get through it with our sanity intact.

At the same time that baseball season started up, I committed to taking time every morning to study the Bible. I had found that I was hit-or-miss in my quiet times, and I wanted to get into a good habit. So every day before I let myself do anything else, I sat down and spent time studying the Word. And you know what? It made an amazing impact on my life, and the life of my family.

Baseball season is nearly over. We have a handful of games left, and our crazy schedule has calmed down. But what could have caused turmoil and stress in our family was actually a really fun time. We were all more connected than ever, had a lot of great times, and even managed to find extra time in there for family nights, exercise, and even a date night or two.

I know that the smooth and basically easy season was a direct result of spending time in the Word every day. I was able to see things more clearly, and above all I had more peace. I found that I was more patient with my kids and my husband, and that there were times when what I read in the morning would run through my mind all day long.

Now, if spending time studying the Bible can make life so much easier and much more bearable even for something as minor as sports, imagine what a difference it can make as we face the really tough challenges that life can and will bring.

Deuteronomy 8:3 states, "So He humbled you, allowed you to hunger, and fed you with manna which you did not know nor did your fathers know that He might make you know that man shall not live by bread alone; but man lives by every word that proceeds from the mouth of the Lord." We need the word of God to live the life that God wants for us.

How the Guide is Laid Out

This guide is separated into short sections that you should be able to get through quickly. I want you to be able to read this and get the information you are looking for, but I want to you to dive into the Bible as quickly as possible. I would rather you spend your time reading God's word than my words. Here are the different chapters, and what you can expect to find in each:

Before You Start – This section contains a few things to keep in mind before you start studying the Bible.

Prayer – In this section I will discuss the importance of prayer, and why you should not try to go through a study of the Bible without spending time talking with God.

Choose the Bible You Want to Use – There are several different translations of the Bible out there, and I know that at times it can get overwhelming. There are some people who are very adamant about what translation is best, but I am not one of those. In this chapter, I will just give you a brief description of the different variations, and hopefully give you the information you need to make the best decision.

Choose the Book You Want to Study – There are 66 different books in the Bible. 39 are found in the Old Testament, which is from the time before Jesus was born, and 27 are in the New Testament, which is from the birth of Jesus forward. Each book has a specific purpose for which it was written, and each one addresses different themes. In this chapter, I will give you a brief outline of what each book is about to help you decide what you want to study.

What to Read When… - Sometimes you may find yourself looking to study part of the Bible that directly addresses whatever you may be going through in your life. I know that there have been many times that I have been in that situation. Whether I was celebrating the birth of a child, frustrated with my life, in mourning, or just plain burnt out, there have been different parts of the Bible that I have clung to in different times. In this section of the guide I will give you an overview of what passages would be appropriate for different scenarios. This is by no means an exhaustive guide, but hopefully will be of use to you.

Move from the Outside In… - This is the section where I will give you the systematic, step-by-step outline to studying the Bible. You will find specific questions to ask yourself as you read and other Bible study tips.

Apply It to Your Life – This is the final section of the guide, and here we will discuss different ways to apply what you learn to your life. It would be a shame to spend all of the time and energy that you put into studying the Bible and not let it change your life. The Bible is not meant to be merely observed or noted. As the verse that I quoted earlier says, it is "living and powerful." Let it change your life.

Seek Wise Counsel – Too many times we try to do everything on our own and think that we can figure it all out. I know that I am guilty of doing this way too often. I don't like to ask for help. But it is very important to seek wise counsel as you are studying the Word. Let other people know what you are up to; especially people who you know love Jesus. Seek out the guidance of people who read and study the Bible. There will most likely be questions that are raised in your mind when you dive into scripture. And that's okay! Just make sure that you find someone to help you find the answers. We were not meant to go through this life alone, and if we try to figure it out on our own, we will get ourselves way off track. That's just the way it goes. God designed us to be in community, so let's do it.

And that's it. It's not a scary or long process. So let's get started!

Chapter 1: Before You Start

There are just a few things that you should take note of before you start studying the Bible. It's not a long list, and don't think that these are prerequisites to reading the Word. You can always read the Bible, whenever you want. These are just a few things that you may want to do and that might make it easier to stay on track.

Things to Do

1. **Announce Your Intentions** – You don't need to make a huge public announcement, start a blog, or even make a Facebook status about the fact that you are going to be studying the Bible. But you do need to let at least a few people know what you are doing, and preferably people who are also studying. This will give you encouragement in what you are doing, and will give you motivation to keep at it. I know that when I am able to discuss whatever I've learned, it makes a deeper impact. My husband and I frequently talk about what we have been reading and learning. Not only does it strengthen our relationship with God, but also with each other. (Just a side note, here. I could probably write an entire guide on this subject – and maybe I will – but I will keep it short. If you are finding someone to discuss this with, unless you are married and it's your spouse, stick with same-sex friends. This prevents too much intimacy and potentially awkward situations. Trust me on this one.)
2. **Find Accountability** – Find someone who you trust and ask them to hold you accountable. All they have to do is ask you if you are reading the Bible. Make sure it is someone who will consistently ask you and someone who you have a strong relationship with. There is no point in finding an accountability partner if you can easily ignore them or even lie to them. This shouldn't be a contentious thing, at all. It is just a lot

easier to keep a commitment if you have someone who is encouraging you to do so.
3. **Set a Time and Place** – Set a specific time every day that you are going to read the Bible. If you like rigid schedules, then be rigid. If you are more relaxed, then set a general time. For me it's when I wake up in the morning. I have my Bible next to my bed, and my goal is that every day before I get up, I read. This works for me because I don't have to be anywhere at any specific time, so I just go with it. A few years ago, though, I had a more rigid schedule and so I had to be more specific with my plans. Whichever way works for you is fine, but just make sure to be intentional about what you are going to do.
4. **Open the Bible** – Just get started! All the plans in the world don't mean anything if you don't actually open the Bible. So put aside excuses, turn off any distractions, and just start reading.

Remember This

- **Find someone you can trust and talk to.** As you read and study the Bible, you will most likely have questions. It will be helpful to have someone that you can go to with any questions. If you can't think of anyone you know who would be able to help you, call a local church! Any pastor would be more than happy to help you.
- **Make studying the Bible a priority.** There are a million other things out there that will try to take your attention away from studying the Bible. Make the Word a priority in your life.
- **Get started.** There's not much more to say about that! Don't just talk about studying the Bible, or read about studying the Bible. Open it up, and get going.

And Don't Forget This

- **Do not try to become an expert.** The point of studying God's word isn't to fill your brain with a bunch of facts. The point is to allow it to transform your life. There are a lot of Bible experts out there, and even they continue to argue about interpretation and trying to understand the mind of God. You don't need to worry about that. Just open the Word, read and study it, and let it change you.
- **Do not make it one more thing to check off of a list.** I love making lists, and I love crossing things off of lists. In fact, the first thing on my to-do list is "Make List" just so I can cross it off when I'm done. But if I view my time studying the Bible as just one more thing that I need to get done, I will not give it the attention that it deserves, and I will not be as open to what the Lord is trying to teach me. I urge you to not view it as one more thing to do, but as a way to discover what God wants for your life. Don't see it as a task, but more as a time to sit and connect with God, to deepen your relationship with him and strengthen your faith.
- **Do not take yourself too seriously.** This is an important thing. Realize that you don't have to be perfect. God just wants you to take the time to read His Word.

See, that's it. Not too long, and not too many things to think about. But just a few guidelines to help you as you being the awesome adventure of studying the Bible.

Chapter 2: Prayer

Why Prayer Matters

Jeremiah 17:9 says, "The heart is deceitful above all things and beyond cure. Who can understand it?" This verse is basically saying that we can deceive ourselves into believing anything. And it's true. We can justify our actions, talk ourselves into things, and we can totally twist the truth so that even if we are completely wrong, we will believe we are right.

Here is a story from my own life. One time I was angry with someone who had wronged me. Looking back on the situation I see that it was right that I was angry. What had happened was definitely not okay. But unfortunately, I did not choose to handle my anger in the way that God wanted me to. I did not glorify Him with my actions, and nothing that I did spoke of Jesus. Rather than praying for the person who hurt me and trying to find resolution to the situation, I chose to gossip as much as possible. I chose to let everyone who would listen know exactly what had happened, and I was nasty. The strangest part about it is that I had convinced myself that what I was doing was right. I had talked myself into thinking that I was just "warning people" or "venting" or, most ridiculously, "sharing a prayer request." I had taken scriptures and twisted them around to seemingly justify my desire for vengeance, and I had deceived myself into believing that I was behaving righteously.

So what does this have to do with prayer? Everything.

Had I been earnestly seeking the Lord in prayer and allowing him to transform my heart, I would have more clearly seen how I should act. If I had prayed and asked Jesus to truly reveal to me the scriptures that would address my situation, I would have been lead to concrete instructions on how to handle everything. But instead I acted on my own, thinking I knew what was best. I did not seek the Lord, and it backfired. I hurt a lot of people, had a lot of apologizing to do, and was deeply embarrassed of my actions.

While prayer is a vital part of everyday life, it is also very important to pray before you begin studying the Bible. You need to ask God to reveal His truth to you. You need to pray that your own agenda, attitudes, and prejudices will be taken out of the way so that you can truly learn whatever it is that God wants you to learn.

One of my favorite things about praying is that the more I do it, the more I realize how awesome God is and how not-awesome I am. When I realize that I can pray to the Creator of the universe and He hears me and wants to help me, I realize that I need His help more than ever. It is a great way to clear my mind and really focus on spending time with Him and reading the Word.

Spending time in prayer is the best way to begin any Bible study. Try it.

Step-By-Step Guide to Prayer

Try to Minimize Distractions – Of course you can talk to God whenever and wherever you are. One of the awesome things about God is that he is everywhere. He can hear over the noise and the clutter of our everyday lives, and he knows what you are thinking. The reason to try to minimize distractions while you are praying is not so that God can hear you better, but so that you can focus more. With four kids running around the house I have a lot of distractions. And there are many times when I pray during the chaos. But there are other times when I need to get away, find a quiet spot, and just focus on talking to Jesus.

Talk to God. – The ability to have a personal relationship with Jesus is amazing. And talking to God is really as simple as just talking. Or even thinking. Or writing. God is always there, and hears you when you call on Him. You don't have to go through any ritual. You don't have to recite anything specific. All you have to do is open your heart and let him know what you are thinking. There are several religions out there that will tell you to chant, or to meditate, or to go through specific rituals to try and get their god to listen and answer. We live and serve the Living God who tells us in Matthew 7:7, "Ask and it will be given to you; seek and you will find; knock and the door will be opened to you."

Ask God to help you understand His word. – Psalm 119:105 says, "Your word is a lamp to my feet and a light for my path." Asking God to help you understand prepares your heart and mind to learn what he has for you, rather than simply relying on your own ideas. The Bible tells us in the book of 1 Kings that Samuel was able to ask the Lord for anything he wanted, and he chose to ask for wisdom. God gave him wisdom, and he was the wisest man who ever lived. James 1:5 promises us that, "If any of you lacks wisdom, you should ask God, who gives generously to all without finding fault, and it will be given to you." So go ahead and ask!

What to Do

Talk to God freely and openly. The One who created the Earth and everything in it hears your prayers. He wants to know what you are thinking and feeling. He already knows, because he created you, but actually speaking to him helps develop an intimacy with the Lord that will strengthen your relationship with him. There is nothing that you cannot tell God.

Tell God what is in your heart and on your mind. You don't have to hold anything back. There is nothing that you can say to him that will make him not love you, and there is nothing that you can say to him that he cannot handle. This has been such a comfort to me in so many times. When I have been angry, I have cried out to God and told him I was angry. I tell him when I'm sad, scared, or lonely. Yes, I praise Him when times are good, but I also let him know what I'm feeling when times aren't as good. I think that too many times we think that we can't tell God the bad stuff. But who better is there to tell?

Be honest. Psalm 119:16 says that, "all the days ordained for me were written in your book before one of them came to be." God already knows what is going on with you, so there is no point in lying to him. Just as with any relationship, being truthful and honest in your prayers will strengthen your relationship with God. And also just as with any relationship, when you aren't being honest, there is a strain in that relationship. There have been times in my own faith where I have just felt like God wasn't there. I thought he was distant, and I didn't know why he had left me. It was only after I was honest with him and admitted what was going on in my life that the distance went away and I felt intimacy with him again. He didn't go anywhere. He was always right there with me. But I had pulled away because I had stopped being honest. Just like it's hard to meet someone's eye when you are lying to them in person, it is hard to look God in the eye, spiritually speaking, when you are lying to God. So just be honest.

<u>What Not To Do</u>

Do not think that you need to perform a specific ritual. I know that I have said this before, but I think it is worth repeating. I know that for a long time I thought that I had to say just the right words or do very specific things in order for God to hear me. I would actually say the same words over and over again and if I didn't I was worried that he wouldn't answer, or even that I would make him angry. It was so freeing to realize that I could talk to him whenever and wherever, and that he would listen. Now I often pray while I am driving in my car, and it's very nice to know that I don't actually have to close my eyes!

Do not be afraid. Don't be afraid that you are going to make God mad. He doesn't want you to tell him what you think you should say, he wants you to be real. As I said earlier, this was a difficult one for me to understand. It was really hard for me to grasp the concept that God is a loving father who wants to hear what is on my mind. He cares about me, and wants me to talk to him.

Do not make it more complicated than it needs to be. Praying is very simple – you just tell God what you want to say. Whether you are thanking him for things, or asking for guidance, or asking for help, or whatever, talk to him like you would a friend. When you get into the habit of praying, you will find that it gets easier and easier. And the more you pray, the more you will want to pray. And sometimes the most powerful prayers are the simplest prayers.

Chapter 3: Choose the Bible You Want to Use

Why there are So Many Bibles

Have you ever gone into a Bible Book Store to try and find a Bible? If you haven't, then make sure you read this section before you do! If you have, then you know what I am talking about. There are walls and walls full of the different types of Bibles, and it can be overwhelming. Here is just a look at the different translations of Bibles out there, and then the different types of Bibles that can be found in each translation. I know that sounds confusing, but stick with me. You'll see what I mean.

Some of the Different Translations

There are countless translations of the Bible, with subtle and not so subtle differences between them. They all say the same thing; it's just how they are worded that changes. I will address some of the main English versions that are available.

King James Version – This version of the Bible is the most widely published version. It was originally published in 1611, and although it has had a few revisions made, it uses Elizabethan English. Think "thy, thee, and thou."

- New King James Version – This is an updated version of the King James Version, using modern English.
- New International Version (NIV) – This version was first published in 1978 and is the most popular version among Evangelical Christians.
- Living Bible – The Living Bible is not a translation of the Bible, but is a paraphrase. This means that the one

who produced it did not look at the original manuscripts, but instead took an already published version of the Bible and then restated what the verses meant.
- New Century Version – This version is based on a Children's Bible. It uses vocabulary that is aimed at younger children and is written with shorter sentences.
- The Message – Although many people believe this to be a paraphrase, it is an actual translation of the Bible. It was created using every day language, with the goal of expressing the way most people think.

Again, there are so many different translations to choose from, but those are the most common ones that you will find. Personally, I use a few different versions. For my daily reading I use an NIV Bible, for in-depth study I use a New King James Bible, and then I also like to read through The Message because it feels like I am reading a novel.

Types of Bibles

Not only do you have all of the different translations to choose from, but within each translation there are different styles of Bibles. And I'm not just talking about hard back or soft back. Here are some types of Bibles:

- **Study Bible** – A study Bible is exactly what it sounds like - a Bible that was created to help people with in-depth study of the word. In a study Bible you will find notes on the different passages, background explanations, charts, maps, and other reference materials.
- **Devotional Bible** – A devotional Bible contains devotional thoughts that you can read along with the scriptures. They will be stories or personal notes to help you better apply the passage to your life. There

are devotional Bibles specifically for men, women, couples, children, youth, athletes, soldiers, and more.
- **Parallel Bible** – A parallel Bible contains different translations of the Bible all side-by-side in one place. This can be very useful when you are studying to try and gain a full understanding of what the verse is saying.

Which Bible Is Best For You?

The best Bible for you is the one that you will read the most! But really, just take a look at the different styles that are out there and see what appeals to you. I actually have all three types of Bibles and several different translations, but the one I use the most often is actually just a plain old Bible that I have had since I was a freshman in high school. There's nothing fancy about it – it's not a study Bible, there are not devotionals on it, and it has a paper cover. But what it has in it are notes and highlighted sections from my personal study over the years. There are times when I see things that I scribbled down when I was a teenager, areas that I highlighted while in college, and things that I am reading through now. Seeing all of it reminds me of my walk with the Lord, and how he has faithfully been with me along the way.

Take some time to look at the different Bibles that are out there. Ask other people what type they like to use. It is largely a matter of personal choice when it comes to choosing a Bible.

Look into it, research it, study it, or just grab the first one you see – whatever your style is, go with it. The most important thing is to get a Bible and start studying!

Chapter 4: Choose the Book You Want to Study

Why Choosing the Book Matters

"I have hidden your word in my heart that I might not sin against you." Psalm 119:11. This is a powerful verse, showing the importance of studying the Bible and what can come from it.

As you are beginning to study the Bible, it is important to carefully choose the book that you will study. There are a few questions that you need to ask yourself:

- What do I want to learn about?
- Am I looking for guidance, encouragement, or a story that would contain a lesson to apply to my life?
- Do I want to study a book in the Old Testament or New Testament?
- What insight am I hoping to gain from this study?

I have a couple of stories about the importance of choosing the book that you are going to be studying. The first happened to me when I was a little girl. I was six or seven years old, and I was in a children's church class while my parents were in their church service. The teachers of the class were new, and no one had really given them much instruction on what they should be teaching their students.

At all.

One of the teachers thought it would be a great idea to study the book of Revelation with this room full of first and second graders. Now, the book of Revelation is full of some great stuff, with prophecy and promises. It gives a detailed account of the John's visions of what will happen at the very end of the world. The book has been carefully studied and many have tried to interpret everything in it to try to find the answer to the question that people have been asking since the day Jesus ascended into Heaven: "When will he be back?" Of course this question is answered in Matthew 24:36 which says, "No one knows about that day or hour, not even the angels in heaven, nor the Son, but only the Father." But this doesn't stop people from trying to figure it out.

Anyway, back to the story. In the book of Revelation, John talks about a lake of fire. And beasts and battles, and other things that are not necessarily appropriate for young children.

But these inexperienced teachers thought it would be funny, and they twisted the Word of God to make it seem like a scary story. I had nightmares for weeks, and it took me years to overcome the idea that the return of our Lord was something to be terrified of.

My second story is related to my first in that it has to do with the same book – Revelation. One summer my husband and I had the pleasure of directing an overnight camp for fourth through sixth graders. We were responsible for leading the campers, as well as the college-aged staff who served as counselors for the younger children.

Well, one week during the summer we had a cabin full of boys who just seemed to be in constant turmoil. In the span of five days they claimed to see UFO's flying in the sky, were certain that one of their bunkmates was possessed by a demon, and were pretty much terrified to leave their cabin once the sun set.

My husband and I were concerned about what was going on with those poor boys. We had both worked with children for several years and had never seen that level of hysteria. One night near the end of camp we were talking with the counselor and trying to help resolve another one of the fear-driven disturbances. At the end of our meeting he said, "Okay, thanks guys. Well, I have to get up there. We're reading through the book of Revelation with these kids."

Suddenly we had a much better understanding of what was going on. The immature counselors who didn't have the knowledge or education to teach the book of Revelation were reading it to a room full of hyper-imaginative, impressionable ten year olds. Thus the ensuing craziness.

Yes, the book of Revelation should be studied. But it is not a book that one should presume to read and understand without question. There are great scholars and theologians that still have not come to a true understanding of what all is contained in those scriptures. And they never will. Churches have split and cults have formed over obsessing and misinterpreting the writings. So if you choose to dive into the book, keep that fact in mind.

Here you will find a step-by-step guide to choosing which book to study. Hopefully this will help you come to a decision about where you want to start.

Step-By-Step Guide to Choosing the Book

1. Decide what you want to learn about. – There are so many amazing stories in the Bible and you will find that each one can be applied to your life in some way or another. Whether you want to learn from the stories of the Israelites traveling in the desert; be inspired by Ruth and her faithfulness and commitment; look at what life was like when Jesus walked upon the earth; or be encouraged and admonished by the letters written by Paul, it's there.
2. Choose whether you want to study a book in the Old Testament, or the New Testament. – Both the Old and

New Testaments contain powerful stories that can change your life. The Old Testament details the time leading up to the birth of Christ, while the New Testament contains stories from his birth forward.
3. Look over the themes of the books and decide which one you are drawn to.
4. Get started! – Don't put it off any longer. The best time to start studying the Bible is right now.

What to Do

- Know that you can learn from whatever you study. The Bible is the inspired word of God and has the power to transform lives.
- Challenge yourself. Have you always only glanced through the Psalms, but completely avoided the New Testament? Or do you only read through the Gospels but ignore the Epistles? If there are parts of the Bible that you have not ever looked at before, challenge yourself. Dive in and see what God has for you.
- Ask for guidance. One of my favorite books in the Bible is the book of Philippians. I have read it countless times, studied it, and taught lessons from it. The very first time I read through the book, I did so because I had asked a friend of mine what would be a good book to read if I need encouragement. She suggested Philippians, and she was right! Ask around and see what books your friends enjoy. You may very well find your new favorite book.

What Not To Do

- Don't be afraid. I don't want you to be afraid that you have to pick the exact perfect book, or that it is possible for you to choose the wrong book to study.

That's not the case at all. If you pray and ask God to lead and guide your study, and to direct you, whatever book you choose will profoundly impact your life.
- Don't limit yourself. Don't feel that you have to choose only one book to study. If you want to look at a book in the Old Testament and then one in the New Testament as well, go for it. There are times when I do that exact thing. I will study an Old Testament Book, a New Testament book, Psalms, and Proverbs, all at the same time. There is no such thing as too much Bible study!
- Don't over-think it. Again, there is no wrong choice. Don't get caught up in this decision, and don't get overwhelmed. Just look at the list, choose one, and get started.

Overview of the Books of the Bible

I know that when you look at the Table of Contents in a Bible and see 66 books listed there it can be confusing, and you may be wondering where you should start. Here is a brief overview of all of the books in the Bible and their themes. This may give you a better understanding of what you are looking at, and help you choose where to start.

Old Testament

- **Genesis** – This book describes the creation of the world. The stories of Adam and Eve, the flood, and Abraham are found here. This is where we are first told of sin entering the world and the relationship between God and his people.

- **Exodus** – The main theme of this book is the character of God while He leads his people out of slavery. We see God taking care of his children, and we see his providence.
- **Leviticus** – The main theme of this book is holiness and learning to try to live a life set apart from sin. We see the laws that God set up for his people to help them live lives that are pleasing to him.
- **Numbers** – This book continues the story of Exodus, and tells of the Israelite's 40 years in the desert. In this book we see that God is serious about what he says and that he will not tolerate sin, but that when we repent he is willing to forgive and have a relationship with us.
- **Deuteronomy** – This book contains the teachings of Moses. In this book he is reminding the Israelites to stay true to God and not fall into idolatry. It was a powerful, relevant message then and it still powerful and relevant today.
- **Joshua** – In this book the Israelite's enter the Promised Land. We see that God is faithful to his Children and forgives us.
- **Judges** – This book describes the different rulers over Israel. It is full of stories of what happens when people try to live without God. There are crazy stories of all kinds of evil, but it also shows what happens when God's people repent.
- **Ruth** – This is the beautiful love story between Ruth and Boaz, and a picture of redeeming love.
- **First and Second Samuel** – These books tell the story of the first kings of Israel, beginning with Saul and then David. In these books we see how God works in the lives of his people, what happens when we obey him, and what happens when we disobey him.
- **First and Second Kings** – These books continue the story of the kings, leading to the division of Israel. In these books we see the lasting consequences of turning from God.

- **First and Second Chronicles** – These books are more historical accounts of the nation of Israel, helping us have a better understanding of God's people and how we all are a part of his plan.
- **Ezra** – This book tells about the Jewish people returning from captivity and rebuilding the temple.
- **Nehemiah** – This book centers on the rebuilding of the city of Jerusalem. In reading this book we can find encouragement in the face of obstacles.
- **Esther** – Ester tells the story of a young woman who acts to stop the slaughter of the Jewish people. We see how God works situations and circumstances so that his will is done, and we also witness that God is faithful to protect his people.
- **Job** – This book addresses suffering and perseverance, and complete reliance upon God. When we study the life of Job we see a man who had every reason to turn his back on God, yet he remained faithful.
- **Psalms** – This is a poetry book, a collection of songs expressing human emotions, from anger to pain to joy. When you study this book you will find examples of everything that you could ever feel. It helps us understand what we are going through, and also to know that no matter what is going on we can trust God and give him praise and honor.
- **Proverbs** – This book contains wise sayings and teachings. Studying this book will help you find practical advice on how to live a life that is pleasing to God, while avoiding the traps that are set for all of us.
- **Ecclesiastes** – This book gets to the heart of what really matters in life… and what doesn't. We see that everything in life should be centered on God, and when it doesn't life is truly meaningless.
- **Song of Solomon** – Although it can be seen only as a love song between husband and wife, it is actually a picture of the love Jesus has for His church. Studying this book can be a wonderful way for a married couple

to learn to express their love and admiration for each other, and it can also be a great way to see the unconditional love of Christ.
- **Isaiah** – In this book the coming of Jesus is prophesied. It was written for God's people who were not living for him. It is a reminder to live our lives in a way that brings honor and glory to God.
- **Jeremiah** – In this book the prophet Jeremiah confronts Israel about their sins, but also points to the coming Savior. When you study this book you will find encouragement to keep seeking God's will for your life. You will see that God does have a plan for your life, and even though there will be times when it is difficult to stay focused, God has you in his hand and will lead and guide you.
- **Lamentations** – This is a book of poetry written because of the fall of Jerusalem. It is a sad book and expressed true angst. Reading this book will help you see that even in our darkest moments we can turn to God.
- **Ezekiel** – This book points out the sin of Israel, but also looks ahead to the restoration of God's people. A study of this book can help you realize that God can turn all situations to his glory and to accomplish his goal – which is a relationship with his people.
- **Daniel** – The story of Daniel and his faith and obedience, and his prophetic visions. In reading this book we see God's power on full display. We see that God is in control and that His will is going to be done.
- **Hosea** – The story of an adulterous wife and her merciful husband, also a picture of God's redemptive love for His people. If you get to the point that you think that God will not love you or forgive you, read this book to be assured of his grace and redemption.
- **Joel** – This book describes the promise of relief that comes when repenting, and also tells of God's awesome power. When you read this book you will see

that God desires to have a relationship with his people.
- **Amos** – This is the story of a man called to tell God's word. In this book we see just how God feels about different issues facing society even today, especially justice.
- **Obadiah** – This is the shortest book of the Old Testament, and it predicts the destruction of the city of Edom. This book will help you understand that ultimately God is in control of everything, and that he will take care of all of us.
- **Jonah** – This book contains the story of Jonah – his calling, disobedience, and his repentance. It also describes the struggles he faces in accepting God's grace. I think that all of us can relate to Jonah and his story. He doesn't want to do what God asks him to do, and he suffers the consequences. Eventually he does follow God's leading, but then manages to quickly forget his own disobedience and falls into the trap of self-righteousness.
- **Micah** – This book contains a call to live lives of worshipful obedience, not merely going through the motions. There are times when we can become discouraged when we look at the sin that runs rampant in the world around us. Reading Micah will help us remember that God is still God, even if everyone around us seems to reject him. We need to follow his commands and desire for our lives, no matter what others are doing.
- **Nahum** – This book addresses the city of Nineveh and shows God's unrelenting desire for His people to honor Him. It brings the promise that God is more powerful than evil, and one day he will destroy evil for good.
- **Habakkuk** – This book discusses God's perfect wisdom and justice. It is a conversation between Habakkuk and God, and we see many of the questions that we have about life being addressed.

- **Zephaniah** – This book talks of punishment and salvation for God's people. When you read this book you will be reminded that although sometimes it may seem as if the darkness in the world will overwhelm, God's love does and will always prevail.
- **Haggai** – This book contains a reminder to put God first in our lives. It can be too easy to let the distractions of the world, or even other commitments that aren't necessarily wrong get in the way of what God wants from us first and foremost: a relationship with him. Reading this book will help you remember to draw near to him first, before anything else in your life.
- **Zechariah** – This book brings a reminder of the coming Messiah and an encouragement to endure during difficult times. A study of this book will help bring hope when it seems like you may be stuck in a rut.
- **Malachi** – This is a call to action to continue to believe, and also look to the coming Messiah. Becoming complacent in our relationship with Christ is a real struggle, and it's not a new one. This issue is addressed in the book of Malachi.
- New Testament
- **Matthew** – One of the four Gospels that tell the story of Jesus, Matthew focuses on God's love for His people and the fulfillment of His promises. It provides the connection between the promised Messiah in the Old Testament and Jesus Christ.
- **Mark** – This book is believed to be based on the teachings of Peter and shows Jesus as a servant. We see a close up look at the suffering Christ endured for us, and get a picture of who Jesus is.
- **Luke** – This book focuses on the grace and mercy of God, and tells the story of Jesus as both fully man and fully God. It is the Gospel that gives us the fullest story of Jesus' ministry while on Earth. When you read this

book you will find more teachings of Jesus and more stories than you will find in the other Gospels.
- **John** – This book contains many of the words of Christ, and describes His perfection, love, mercy, and sacrifice. In this book you will find sermons that Jesus preached which were not recorded in any of the other Gospels.
- **Acts** – Sometimes called "The Acts of the Apostles," this book describes the beginning of the Christian church. We pick up as Jesus is taken into Heaven, and then we get to read about what his followers did who were left behind. We see as the church grows, faces persecution, and ultimately how lives are changed because of following Jesus. I love studying the book of Acts because it is so encouraging to see how these men who walked with Jesus didn't sit around confused after they left, but were filled with the power of the Holy Spirit to continue his work, work which continues today.
- **Romans** – This is a letter from Paul written to the Church in Rome. It discusses the need for a Savior and the work completed by Jesus on the cross. This book gives a clear picture of the saving grace of Jesus and points out that it has nothing to do with us or anything we do, but it's all about Christ.
- **First and Second Corinthians** – Letters written to the Church in Corinth, these books address what it means to live as a follower of Christ. Paul had started the church here, and then a few years later was hearing news that there were some serious issues creeping into the church and corrupting it. It should not be surprising that the issues they were facing then are still the exact same issues we face today. We can look to this book to see how we are to address specific situations.
- **Galatians** – In this book Paul tells of God's grace and the sufficiency of Jesus. Written to address some issues and false teachings that had crept into the

church in Galatia, we can definitely find answers to questions that arise today.
- **Ephesians** – This book discusses the body of Christ, referring to the body of believers. When you read this book you will see that God has an awesome plan for your life, and a calling on your life to live set apart from the world. There are so many mixed messages out there about who you should be or what you should strive for, but Paul addresses these issues in this book. We see that we shouldn't let the world define who we are, but instead our identity should come only from being a lover of Jesus.
- **Philippians** – Written while Paul was in jail, this book discusses joy and the example of humility shown by Christ. This is probably my favorite book in the Bible. All of them are awesome, obviously, because they are all God's word, but Philippians is the one I find myself turning to most often. It gives a picture of how we are to live, and gives encouragement to keep striving to live that way. We see that we don't need to worry about anything that we may be facing in our lives, and that we can truly go to God with it all and trust that he will work it all out. This book gives the admonishment to live a life full of joy and peace, knowing that our lives are different because of our relationship with Jesus.
- **Colossians** – This book addresses false doctrine and gives instruction to resist lies and return to the truth of Christ. Paul wrote this book to people who were being taught things that were contrary to the Gospel. He set them straight, and his words are ones that are relevant today. We are surrounded by false teachers and liars, and we need to cling to the truth.
- **First and Second Thessalonians** – These books serve as a reminder to live lives that are pleasing to God. The believers in Thessalonica were surrounded by the same temptations that we are surrounded by today. These books help give a better of

understanding on how we are to view our world, and help remind us to focus on Christ and remember that this is not our home. We are to seek to serve God and not get distracted by the temporary pleasures that may entice us.

- **First and Second Timothy** – Written to a young pastor, these books give advice on how to care for and run a church. Don't think that this book is just for leaders of the church, though. Anyone who is a part of a body of believers can read these books and gain insight on how the church was designed to function.
- **Titus** – This book also contains instructions for churches. It shouldn't really come as a surprise that it is tough to run a church. Think about it for a minute – you have a group full of people who are trying to figure out what it means to follow Jesus, all coming together to try to serve him and honor him, while dealing with personalities that don't always mesh. Titus faced the same issues, and the instructions that are given to him can be applied to anyone.
- **Philemon** – Although it is a short letter, this book paints a beautiful picture of forgiveness and restoration. It centers on a runaway slave who is returning to his homeland, but Paul urges the people to accept him as an equal, and forgive him for leaving.
- **Hebrews** – Written to a group of people considering returning to Judaism from Christianity, this book discusses the saving grace and perfection of Christ. It was very difficult for the early believers to follow Christ, and it was very tempting for them to renounce their beliefs to put an end to the persecution they were facing. Paul encouraged them to keep true to their faith. You may not face the same struggles as these early believers did, but there are times when it is difficult to follow Christ, and you will be tempted to just give up. Reading Hebrews will help you find the encouragement and motivation you need to stay focused.

- **James** – This book gives instructions on what it means to live as a follower of Christ. Reading this book helps you gain a better understanding of how to take your faith and let it transform the way you live. A lot of times it can be easy to say that we believe things, yet when it comes down to changing our attitudes and actions it is more difficult. James gives us practical advice and instructions on how to live out what we say we believe.
- **First and Second Peter** – These books discuss courage in the face of trials, and give a reminder to resist false teaching. Peter wrote these books to Christians who were undergoing severe persecution. Surrounded on all sides by people who hated them, the audience of these books faced torture and death because of their faith. Peter gives encouragement that we can get through any trials that we face, and to realize that when they come they will serve to strengthen our relationship with Christ and bring glory and honor to him. These books give a good reminder that this world is temporary, and our real home is in Heaven with Jesus. It is easier to face anything that comes our way in this life when we keep that perspective.
- **First, Second, and Third John** – These books discuss relationships, with both God and other believers. One of the most difficult things we can face is learning how to deal with other people. I know that as a parent I often find myself struggling to not be impatient with my children, and in my marriage my husband and I are constantly working on putting each other first and not letting petty issues divide us. These books help remind us that our first and most important relationship is with God, and we are to use that relationship as a foundation and guide for all of our other relationships. God loves us, and we are to love others. It is not always easy, but it is simple.

- **Jude** – This book gives stern reminders to remain unified and to live moral lives. It is a rather stern book, but the message is one that we all need to hear. We live in a world where the seemingly gray areas in regard to moral behavior keep getting larger, but God's word has not changed at all. It can be easy to make small compromises and slowly walk away from what the Bible teaches. Jude serves as a wakeup call to get us back on track.
- **Revelation** – This book contains stern letters of warning to churches who have lost their way, and also prophecies of God's ultimate victory over evil. This is a good book to read when you feel like evil is always winning and that there is no hope. We see in this book that ultimately God triumphs and there will be a full restoration with him, and we will worship him face to face.

Those are the books of the Bible. Each one is inspired by God and written for us to read and learn.

Take some time to look over the different books, and pray about which one you want to start with. Again, there's no wrong place to start. Wherever you read you can be sure that if you ask God to use it to change your life, he will.

If you have something specific that you are wanting to read about, go to the next section. In there I will discuss what passages would be helpful for very specific things that you may be facing in your life.

Chapter 5: What to Read When

Whenever I look back on my relationship with God, I am amazed to see how he has been there no matter what I have been going through in my life. When things have been going well and I have seen him actively working in and through me, I have been able to praise him and draw near to him. When things have been tough and I have wondered where he is, I see now that he used those times to refine my faith, and also to pull me closer than I ever realized I was. That is to me one of the most awesome aspects of having a real relationship with a Living God.

One of the things that I have realized also is that I have different passages or books that I turn to at different times in my life. I have already mentioned how fond I am of the book of Philippians but there are others that I go to frequently. When I feel like giving up on my responsibilities as a wife and mom, I turn to Proverbs 31 for encouragement and inspiration. When I am angry and wanting to tear people down, I turn to James. When I am hurting I look to Psalms, and when I want to be encouraged in my faith I look to stories in Daniel or Samuel.

Those are just a few examples of the different passages I use. Several years ago someone gave me a book that was all about what passages to read at different times in my life. It was a very helpful book, and I wanted to create something similar for you. So here you go!

What to Read When You are Feeling...

I often hear emotions being criticized by people. How often have you heard someone being described as "too emotional?" I know that I hear it all the time, and it frustrates me. I don't think that there is such a thing as "too emotional." I think that the problem comes when we allow ourselves to be ruled by our emotions, making decisions and interacting with people solely based on how we may be feeling at the moment.

The truth is, God created our emotions. He gave us the capacity to feel, and to feel deeply. And there is nothing that we will experience that he has not experienced himself, and that he does not understand. The great news is that no matter how we feel, we will find it addressed in the Bible.

What to Read When You are Sad

There are many situations that can and will cause you to feel sadness. It may be a particular event or circumstance, or it may just be a combination of factors making you feel this way. I know that there are times when I feel sad, but I don't know exactly what is making me sad. Whatever the cause, I trust in the fact that I can turn to the word.

- **1 Peter Chapter 1** – All of 1st Peter is a great book to read any time, but Chapter 1 is especially helpful when you are feeling sad. In this chapter Peter reminds us that first and foremost this world is not our true home. We belong to Heaven, and when we have that perspective the trials that surround us often don't seem as overwhelming. Peter also instructs us that although the trials we are facing right now are difficult and not necessarily something we enjoy, we can rest in the knowledge that there is a definite purpose for them. We can know that the trials are strengthening and refining our faith, and God will use everything to draw us closer to him and to bring him glory and honor.
- **Psalm 22** – When a passage starts out with the words, "My God, my God, why have you forsaken me?" you know that it will be helpful when you are

feeling down. I love this Psalm because the author is clearly distraught, but he cries out to God and in doing so surrenders himself to God's authority, and remembers that God is holy and awesome. He takes his focus off of himself and instead turns to God and praises him, and in doing that he finds the peace that he is so desperately seeking. If you read and study this Psalm and allow yourself to go through the same process, you will find a similar result.
- **John 14** – This chapter begins with the words of Jesus telling us, "Let not your heart be troubled." That is exactly what I want to hear when I am feeling sad! This passage takes us to Jesus, and we hear what he has to say to us. We know his love for us, and we see that his desire is for us to feel peace and comfort. I love knowing that I have a Savior who cares deeply for me.

What to Read When You are Angry

Wouldn't it be great if we lived in a world where we never had to worry about feeling angry? Unfortunately, that's not the case. I know that there are things that make me angry a lot, both huge things and little things. Whatever it is that is causing me to feel this way, I know that I can turn to scripture to help me work through it.

- **Matthew 5:21-24** - This passage takes us right to Jesus and what he says about how we should treat other people. I know that it is not a fun thing to hear that we need to love others, even those who have wronged us, but it's the truth. It is good to deal with our anger honestly and to know that God does not want us to let it sit and fester and turn us bitter.
- **Psalm 37:1-11** – When I am angry and read this passage I am reminded of the essential truth that God

will not stand for evil. But I am also encouraged to not spend time dwelling on the things that I cannot change or control and instead focus on what I can do, which is turn my heart and mind towards God. This passage helps put things into perspective, and it is a welcome perspective, especially when I am angry.

- **James 1** – This is another passage that may not be comfortable to read when you are angry, but it will definitely be helpful. In this passage James is giving instructions on how we are to live, and points us to the responsibility that we must take for our own actions. I know that there have been several times when I have been angry but knew that there was nothing that I could do about the situation. And instead of committing myself to God and letting him change my heart and my attitudes, I let myself get caught up in the emotions that I was feeling. If we heed James' instruction to "be swift to hear, slow to speak, slow to wrath," how much of a difference are we going to feel? And how much of an impact will it make on the way that we behave?

What to Read When You are Happy

When I talk with people I find that a lot of times they fall into one of two categories: Either they find that it is easy to turn to God and have a relationship with him when times are good but when times are bad they get angry and don't want to turn to him, or it's the opposite. But God is with us through the good and the bad, and we can and should praise him no matter what we are facing. Here are some great passages to read when you are really happy:

- **Psalm 92** – The first verse of this Psalm pretty much sums it up: "It is good to give thanks to the Lord, and to sing praises to your name, O Most High." This chapter walks through a series of praises and shouts to God, ending with the thought that, "He is my rock, and there is no unrighteousness in him." This is a great way to praise the Lord, and I find it an excellent way to begin a day.

- **1 Samuel 2:1-10** – In this passage we see Hannah praising God for giving her a son. Hannah had been barren and the Lord heard her cry and blessed her. This prayer helps us see all what the Lord has done, all that he is doing, and all that he will continue to do. The next time that you are feeling exceedingly blessed, study this passage and join Hannah in crying out to God.
- **Psalm 150** – If you want to praise the Lord and find encouragement and different ways to praise him, this is the chapter for you! The author starts out by letting us know that everyone and everything should praise the Lord, and then gives several examples of how to do this. I love this passage because it shows that God doesn't want us to be solemn and formal in expressing our joy and adoration for him. He calls for loud cymbals, the sound of the trumpet, and dancing. There are times when I wonder why we can be so loud and borderline out of control when we go to sporting events yet seem to feel the need to be more reserved when expressing our thoughts and feelings about God. This Psalm shows us that this isn't the case and that we are free to worship the Lord without reservation.

What to Read When You Feel Like Giving Up

Let's be honest here. There are times when you are going to feel like giving up. I know that I face that, and I have yet to meet someone who never feels like giving up on striving to live a life that is pleasing to God. It can be very tough, especially with temptations surrounding us. But we shouldn't give up. We need to keep going forward, trusting that God will get us there. Here are some great passages to read when the thought of sticking it out seems impossible.

- **Philippians 1** – Yes, it's my favorite book. But this passage is so encouraging because we see what Paul prayed for his fellow believers. We can pray the same things. And we see the promise that, "He who has begun a good work and you will complete it until the day of Jesus Christ." Paul gives instructions on how to live, and we see that it is worth it to keep pressing forward, and to know that God will get us through. Paul shows us through his own example that there is nothing that we shouldn't be willing to endure for the cause of Christ. Knowing that Paul wrote this book while he was being held in chains because of preaching the Gospel really helps put things in perspective.
- **1 Kings 19:4-16** – I know that sometimes all I want to know is that I am not alone in whatever I am going through. I want to know that someone else has been there, and that there is an example for me of how to get through it. When you read this passage in 1 Kings you will see that Elijah felt like giving up. But you will also see that God ministered to him and gave him the encouragement that he needed to not give up. We can trust in the fact that God will do the same for us. He knows our hearts and he knows what we are going through, and he will get us through it.
- **Psalm 20** – This Psalm begins with the words, "May the Lord answer you in the day of trouble; may the name of the God of Jacob defend you." When I feel like giving up it is because I have lost sight of the fact that whatever I am facing will pass, and that God will work things out. This passage gives us a clear reminder that God is in control and will hear our prayer. Don't give up. Turn to him, trust in him, and

know that he is with you, no matter how bleak things may seem.

What to Read When You are Sick

I have just recently come through a very bad illness. I was sick for about six months, and it took me four months to fully recover. The illness affected my ability to think, and since I make my living as a writer, this caused some serious issues in my family. Even right in the middle of everything, I knew that God was there with me. I knew that he would work everything out for his glory. Now that we are past that intense time, I can see how God was there helping us, and I see the good that has come out of it. Here are some verses to read when you are sick that may help make it a little bit easier to handle:

- **James 5:14–15** – This passage starts out with asking, "Is anyone among you sick?" Well there you go – specific instruction on what to do when you are sick. It should not surprise you that the action to take is prayer. In these verses we are instructed to go to people to have them pray for us. I know that it took a long time for me to be willing to ask people to pray for me when I was sick. I have a very strong personality, and I like to give off the impression that I can do anything and everything. I don't like to feel week, I certainly don't want to let others know that I am struggling. What I found, though, is that when I got to the point where I humbled myself and admitted my struggle, I found peace and encouragement. It was awesome to have people around me to lift me up in prayer, and it was also nice to have people walk alongside us and help us out. I found that even though God did not immediately heal my sickness, he gave me the strength and grace I needed to endure it.

- **Philippians 4:4-7** – This passage starts with the instruction to "Rejoice in the lord always." This may seem strange to you to think about rejoicing in your sickness, but it isn't strange at all. Taking time to praise God in the midst of our trials helps take our eyes off of what we are going through and turn them to where we need to be. The passage goes on to tell us to pray, and then promises that when we do we will receive the peace that can come only from God. This peace is one of the things that stands out the most for me from what I experienced during my most recent illness. There were times when everything around me seemed so dark, and a lot of people around me were wondering how we were going to get through it, and I know that the overwhelming peace of God is the only thing that sustained us.
- **Isaiah 40:27-31** – The last verse in this passage sums it all up, "But those who wait on the Lord shall renew their strength; they shall mount up with wings like eagles, they shall run and not be weary, they shall walk and not faint." We can look to this passage to find the reminder that God will lift us up no matter what. God is bigger than everything, bigger than any illness we may be facing. Putting trust in him will help us to know and rest assured that God is in control. If he heals us, it will be only because of him and we will praise him for it. If he chooses not to heal us, we will know that he is going to use us for his purpose and to do his will, and we will praise him for it. No matter what, he will give us the strength that we need.

What to Read When You are Lonely

I don't like to feel lonely, and I am thankful that it doesn't happen very often. But there are times when I have felt that way. It has always surprised me that even though I am surrounded by people, I can feel alone. In fact, I recently felt incredibly lonely, even though I was living in a house with eleven other people! But there are times when we feel like we have no one else to turn to, no one who understands where we are, and no one who relates to us. When we feel this way we should turn to God and allow him to fill the void. Here are some passages that may help in that regard.

- **Psalm 25** - This may seem trite, but sometimes the greatest help when you are feeling lonely is to know that you are not alone. In verse 16 of this Psalm the author states, "Turn yourself to me, and have mercy on me, for I am desolate and afflicted." In studying this chapter we see that even when everything seems hopeless, it is possible to praise the Lord and turn our eyes to him. I love that this Psalm starts out with pointing us straight to God. It is very true that there is nothing that we can do on our own, and the sooner we turn to the Lord for help, the better off we will be.
- **John 13:1-17** – I know that sometimes when I feel lonely the best thing that I can do is turn my attention to other people, and serve them. In this particular passage we see Jesus serving his disciples, to the point of washing their feet. If we follow the lead of Christ and put others before ourselves, we will be blessed. I know that when I reach out to other people, I not only experience a strengthening of my relationship with those people, but my relationship with God is stronger. It also changes the way that I view things. I no longer feel like I am all alone, but instead I look around to see who I can reach out to next.
- **Matthew 28:16-20** – In this passage we see Jesus with his disciples after he has risen from the dead. I love this section because Jesus knows that he is going to be going up into Heaven, and so he uses the time to tell the disciples the things that they need to hear, and words that I am sure they clung to for the rest of their lives. He knew that they were going to face difficult

times; he knew that they were going to be afraid; and he knew that they were going to feel lonely. So what did he tell them? In verse 20 he says, "Lo, I am with you always, even to the end of the age." This promise was not only for his disciples. This is for all of us. We can claim the truth that Jesus is with us always. We can know that no matter what is happening, we are never alone.

What to Read during this Major Life Event…

Do you have anyone who you can think of who has been by your side during the major events in your life? I do. I can think of a few select people who have shared with me in my graduation from high school and college, were there when my husband gave me a promise ring, were actively involved in my wedding, and who talked to me when I had my children. I have rejoiced with these people in the good times, and I have cried with these same people during the difficult times.

As much comfort as these friends of mine have brought, it is nothing compared to the peace that has come from knowing that God was with me during all of it, and that there were passages in the Bible that specifically addressed whatever I was going through. It reinforced the fact that God created me, knows everything that will happen to me before it ever happens, and has given me all the tools that I will need to handle whatever comes my way.

Here are some passages to study during the major life events that you may face. Diving into the Word will help make the rejoicing even more exciting, and will bring comfort when you mourn.

What to Read When You are Starting College

I remember when I started college like it was yesterday, although it was a lot longer ago than I really want to admit! But I remember that I was excited and scared all at the same time. I know that once I got to the school and started moving my things into my room, all I wanted to do was focus on the task at hand. I was meeting knew people and trying to get everything situated, all while trying to avoid the truth hanging over my head that I had moved out of my home. Once all of the work was finished and there was nothing left to do but say goodbye, I had the strangest sensation. I will never forget the way that I felt watching my parents leave. Here are some passages that really helped me get through that strange yet exciting time:

- **Joshua 1** – I think that this chapter is one of the best passages that someone who is starting college could ever read. It begins with God telling Joshua to go in and claim the Promised Land. Joshua had grown up hearing about this Land, knowing the promise that one day it would belong to him and his people, and now he was given the monumental task of making this happen. God knows what Joshua is feeling when he receives this instruction and gives him words of comfort. In verse 9 God tells Joshua, "Have I not commanded you? Be strong and of good courage; do not be afraid, nor be dismayed, for the Lord your God is with you wherever you go." We can claim these same words no matter where we are going. When we venture out into new territory, we can know that the Lord is with us wherever we go.
- **1 and 2 Timothy** – These books were written specifically to a young person. Paul wrote them to encourage Timothy, a young pastor. Paul knew the struggles and temptations that Timothy would face, and his instructions are excellent ones to take to

heart, no matter what your field of study may be. 1 Timothy 4:12 is especially helpful, and it says, "Let no one despise your youth, but be an example to the believers in word, in conduct, in love, in spirit, in faith, in purity." How many students at college campuses would be classified as examples of faith or purity? I know the number isn't huge, but that does not mean that it needs to stay that way! How awesome would it be to see young men and women standing up for Jesus on their campuses? Another great passage is 2 Timothy 2:22 which says, "Flee also youthful lusts; but pursue righteousness, faith, love, peace with those who call on the Lord out of a pure heart." Another excellent reminder for college students in particular, but everyone should heed this instruction.

- **Philippians 4:10-13** – I include these verses not just because they are found in my favorite book, but because they are ones that can be especially encouraging to college students. Many people have heard verse 13 taken out of context. We see the words, "I can do all things through Christ who strengthens me," and many people have twisted this to justify all kinds of dangerous and reckless behavior. But the verse comes at the end of this passage where Paul is talking about the fact that he has learned to live in poverty and in wealth, and he is saying that he can be content no matter what his financial situation, because of Christ who strengthens him. Now, I know that when I was in college my financial situation was bleak. And I know that I am not the only one who experienced this. But looking to the Word for encouragement is a great reminder that it really doesn't matter how much money we have or don't have, but that we can thrive in any situation because we have Christ in us and he strengthens us.

What to Read When You are Falling in Love

I dated a lot when I was younger. This isn't a boast, nor is it a shameful admission – it's merely fact. When I met my husband though, I knew that it was all different. My mom, however, was a bit skeptical when I got engaged. She had seen different guys in my life, and she wanted to know what was different about this man. She asked me, "Why do you want to marry him?" And I gave her the simple answer, "Because I'm in love with him." And that was all she needed to know.

I was not one to use the words "love" or "falling in love" loosely. I was very guarded with my heart, and I knew that once I fell in love, I would be in love for the rest of my life. Now, a lot of that conviction was naiveté. I now know that the being in love feeling isn't always there, and that sometimes it's just plain commitment that keeps my marriage going during the times when love might not be the first word that comes to mind when I think of my husband. But nevertheless, we were young, and I was in love.

You may have a different experience than me. You may have fallen in love several times, or you may still be waiting for the person with whom you will spend the rest of your life. No matter what your situation, you should turn to the Bible for direction in matters of love. In fact, it's the only place you should turn. There are so many other voices out there that give horrible advice on love, but they all seem legitimate on the surface, so it is easy to get led astray. Cling to the Bible. Don't follow your heart. Don't do what feels right. Look to the Word for a true and unchanging view on love.

Here are some places you may want to start:

- **1 Corinthians 13** – This is called "the love chapter," and for good reason – it talks all about love. It gives us a picture of what true love is, and what true love is not. True love means sacrificing yourself for another person, wanting what is best for someone else, and being willing to forgive. God created love and he gave us the ultimate picture of love in Jesus Christ. If we want our love relationships to last we need to make sure that they are centered and focused on Christ, and that the love that we are exhibiting is the type of love described in this passage.

- **Romans 6** – Yes, you are in love. Yes, this person is the person that you have dreamed of spending the rest of your life. And yes, this person awakes desires in you that you did not know you could ever have. But no, that does not mean that God's standard for sexual relationships has changed. God designed sex to be between a husband and a wife. And that's it. So until you are married, you need to abstain. Romans 6 will help remind you that our body is to be used to glorify and honor God. I don't want you to be discouraged here and think that there is no way that you will be able to withstand the temptation. 1 Corinthians 10:13 tells us that, "No temptation has overtaken you except such as is common to man, but God is faithful, who will to allow you to be tempted beyond what you are able, but with the temptation will also make the way of escape, that you may be able to bear it."
- **Colossians 3:12-17** – When you are first falling in love it is easy to treat your beloved with respect, honor, kindness, and patience. But as you get past those early stages and start becoming comfortable and in sync with your best friend, it becomes easier to let your guard down. You don't feel like you have to try as hard, and things that are not loving can start to creep into your relationship. Studying this passage in Colossians can be an excellent reminder of the way that we are supposed to live. Paul reminds us of the qualities that we are supposed to exhibit, and then in verse 14 tells us, "but above all these things put on love, which is the bond of perfection." I wish that I

could say that I was always the picture of compassion and grace, but that's just not the case. These verses, though, grab my attention and remind me who I am in Christ and how I should be acting.

What to Read When You are Getting Married

Congratulations, you are getting married! This is a very exciting time in your life, and one that I am sure is full of more emotions than you knew you were capable of. I want to make sure, though, that with all of the preparations for the Wedding Day you don't lose sight of this very important truth: It is only one day. While the day of your wedding is one that you and your spouse will never forget, the majority of your time and energy right now should be going into preparing for your marriage. You know, the rest of your life.

There are shelves full of books on how to make a marriage last. Millions and millions of dollars are poured into helping people discover what it takes to have a marriage that thrives. But if we aren't looking to the Bible for guidance, we are looking in the wrong places. It's as simple as that.

- **Ephesians 5:22-33** – In this passage Paul gives specific advice to husbands and wives. He tells us what it takes for a Christian marriage to thrive. The final verse pretty much sums it all up with these words, "Nevertheless let each one of you in particular so love his own wife as himself; and let the wife see that she respects her husband." I'm not going to say that marriage is easy. It takes hard work, commitment, dedication, and sacrifice. I will say, though, that a marriage that is built on the foundation of Christ and one that keeps him in the center is a whole lot easier. My husband and I have had our ups

and downs, for sure. But when we are both studying the Word, praying together, praying for each other, and seeking to honor God in our marriage, it is all so much better.
- **Song of Solomon** – This is the ultimate love poem. It is a celebration of the physical love between a man and a wife. God created love, God created marriage, and God created sex. When it is all used to bring glory and honor to him, it is a beautiful thing.
- **Proverbs 31-10-31** – Here we find the description of a virtuous wife. We see the qualities and traits of a woman who loves the Lord and allows him to work in her life and use her to bless her husband, her children, and those around her. Although many see this as just a passage for women, I see it as a beautiful picture of marriage that honors God. Her husband blesses her and encourages her and helps her be the woman that she is created to be, and she in turn honors her husband and helps make him a better man. It's a picture that I strive to emulate in my own home, fully aware of the fact that the only way that it is accomplished is through Christ.

What to Read When You are Having Children

I love my children. I have four of them, three boys and a girl. I did not enjoy being pregnant though. I was sick as a dog, and each pregnancy got progressively worse, until I spent the last two months of my last pregnancy on bed rest. What I did enjoy while being pregnant though was anticipating what it would be like when I met my child for the first time. With my oldest, I was scared that I was going to make mistakes and not know how to be a mom. But I was also excited, and couldn't believe that God had chosen me to be someone's mother. With my second, I was nervous about what would happen to our family dynamic, but I was happy to bring another little one into our home. With my third and fourth it was the same mixture of fear and joy, all rolled up together.

I cherish the Bible passages that I read during my pregnancies. I hear them now and it takes me back to those days and I am amazed to see how far I have come since then.

I know that during the time I was expecting, my husband also leaned on the Lord. Not too long ago he found a passage that he had read the day after our oldest was born. He read it to our family which now contained four children, and it was overwhelming to see where the Lord had brought us from that day.

Bringing children into your family is a major life event and not one that should be taken lightly. But just like with all of the other life events, when we seek the Lord's guidance he will bring us through it.

- **Matthew 19:13-15** – This passage is to me the essence of what my life as a parent is all about. In it we see that Jesus was surrounded by children who were trying to come to him, and his disciples tried to keep them from him. The disciples were clearly missing the point, thinking that Jesus was too busy or too important to have time for little messy, loud, annoying, obnoxious, crying, whining children. But Jesus put his disciples into their place, and said, "Let the little children come to me, and do not forbid them; for of such is the kingdom of heaven." My first responsibility as a parent is to bring my children to Jesus. It is my duty to tell them about Christ. It is my duty to model Jesus for them. The last thing that I want to do is to get in the way of my children and their relationship with God. I pray that Jesus would use me to draw my children closer to him. It is an honor and something that I take very seriously.

- **Psalm 139** – This Psalm talks about the fact that God knew all of us before we were born and that he was the one to knit us together while we were in the womb. It talks about how his thoughts of us are so vast that we cannot even begin to comprehend them all, and that there is nowhere that we can go where he will not be with us. I know that this is a very helpful passage for me to read when I am dealing with my children. I love them to pieces. They are fun, smart, caring, and extremely energetic kids. But there are times that they drive me nuts. In an instant the fun can turn to reckless, the smart can turn to sassy, the caring can turn to nosy, and the energetic can turn to rebellious. In those times I need to be reminded that God created them and they are perfectly made. My job is to help shape them and guide them into who they will be, trusting God to work in their hearts and lives. Studying this passage helps give me the perspective that at times I so desperately need.
- **Ephesians 6:1-4** – Just as Ephesians 5 gives specific instructions for husbands and wives, this passage gives instructions for parents and children. I need to teach my children the first verse which instructs them to obey their parents, but I also need to take verse 4 to heart. This verse says, "And you, fathers, do not provoke your children to wrath, but bring them up in the training and admonition of the Lord."

<u>What to Read When You Have Lost a Loved One</u>

When I was seven months pregnant with my youngest child and confined to bed, I lost my beloved grandfather. He was a wonderful man who loved the Lord with his whole heart and served him faithfully in ministry for over fifteen years. My Papa was my role model, my strongest supporter, and a man

I greatly admired. At the end of his life he suffered from ALS and when he went to meet Jesus face to face, while we were all sad to lose him, there was comfort in the fact that he was no longer in pain.

Although there was that comfort, it was still horrible to lose him. Death is not natural. It was one of the consequences of sin entering in the world, and we never will, nor should we ever, feel comfortable with death. Even though he has been gone for over three years, there are still times when the loss feels like it just occurred yesterday. I will see or hear something that reminds me of him, and suddenly I will find myself crying.

God knows our hearts and knows how we feel when we lose a loved one, and he has given us scriptures to help us during this most difficult time.

- **1 Thessalonians 4:13-18** – This passage addresses the fact that when people who love Jesus die, they go to be with him. It also tells us that when Jesus returns, he will bring those who have died with him. This is the comfort that we will see our loved ones again, when we are all made whole and perfect in Christ. I will see my Papa again, and I will see him without pain and suffering. We will worship our savior together, without the pain and trials of this earthly life. This is a promise that brings me hope and joy.
- **Romans 8:35-39** – This passage tells us that nothing, not even death, can separate us from the love of God. When you have lost a loved one and everything in your world seems like it has been turned upside down, it is so comforting to know that the constant of God's love is always there. He is with you during your grief, and only he can give you the peace and comfort you seek.

- **Jeremiah 31:1-14** – One of the most helpful things to remember when you are overwhelmed with grief is that it is not going to stay this way forever. We are given the promise that God will make all things new. Verse 13 of this passage says, "I will turn their mourning to joy, will comfort them, and make them rejoice rather than sorrow." God will bring healing through all of this.

I hope that this list will be of help to you when you are facing specific situations in your life. It is by no means exhaustive, but my prayer is that it serves as a good jumping off point for you.

Chapter 6: Move From the Outside In

Let's take a few moments to look at a practical, step-by-step guide to studying the Bible. It doesn't have to be an exact scientific approach, but just think about it as starting from the outside and moving in.

Step-By-Step

1. **Pray.** Yes. Starting with prayer is the best way to begin your study of the Bible. You need to ask him to open your heart and your mind, and to reveal his truth to you. Ask God to help silence your own preconceived ideas of what is right so that you can truly learn from Scripture. Psalm 63:1 says, "Oh God, you are my God; early will I seek you; my soul thirsts for you; my flesh longs for you in a dry and thirsty land where there is no water." This verse shows us that we need God's guidance. We need him to lead us and to show us things. Our souls long for him and without him we have nothing. Don't forget to seek him first as you look to his Word.
2. **Choose the passage.** Choose whatever scripture you want to learn about. I have given you an overview of the different books of the Bible, as well as specific passages that you can read at different times in your life. But if none of that jumps out at you, ask someone that you trust what they would recommend studying. Remember, there is no wrong place to start. After all, as it says in 2 Timothy 3:16-17, "All Scripture is given by inspiration of God, and is profitable for doctrine, for reproof, for correction, for instruction in righteousness, that the man of God may be complete, thoroughly equipped for every good work." And also

we see in Isaiah 55:11 that, "So shall my word be that goes forth from my mouth; it shall not return to me void, but it shall accomplish what I please, and it shall prosper in the thing for which I sent it." So choose what you want to study, and get started.

3. **Consider the book.** Now that you have chosen the passage, take a while to learn why the book was written in the first place. As I mentioned earlier, a lot of Study Bibles have introductions at the beginning of each book to tell you the purpose of the book. If not, look online for explanations of why the book was written. Doing this will help you gain a better understanding of the point the author is trying to make. For example, we know that the books of 1 Peter and 2 Peter were written to people who were experiencing unbelievable persecution. They were hated by everyone, and the threat of death was real and constant. Reading the books with that in mind helps bring a whole new light to what Peter is saying.

4. **Consider the culture.** Do a bit of research into what the culture of the time was when the passage was written. Was it during a time of war? Was it a wealthy culture? Were there specific areas of concern that needed to be addressed? Again, if your Bible doesn't have this information included, take the time to look it up. This step is important so that you will know that the instructions found within the text are not arbitrary, but instead were written for a specific purpose. When I looked up the culture of the Philippi, the setting of the church in my favorite book Philippians, I learned that it was a wealthy area. This made it much more meaningful to me when Paul is talking about the sufficiency of Christ and that no matter what financial situation you find yourself in, it is all possible because of Jesus.

5. **Apply it to today.** Once you learn the culture of that time, take that knowledge and apply it to today. The technology and appearances may be different, but the

same issues can be found in any society. Look around and consider what similarities there are, and how the verses apply in today's world. As we are told in Ecclesiastes 1:9, "That which has been is what will be, that which is done is what will be done, and there is nothing new under the sun." Whatever trials or circumstances you are facing today, you will find people in the Bible who were facing the same core situations.

6. **Make it personal.** Now comes the tough part. Look into your own life and see how what you have just read can impact your thoughts, attitudes, ideas, beliefs, or actions. Don't walk away from it thinking that there is nothing for you. See what you can learn, and put it into action.

Try to remember those six steps every time you study the Bible. They can help you get a fuller picture of the Word of God and can help transform your life.

Chapter 7: Apply It To Your Life

1 Corinthians 13: 1-3 says, "Though I speak with the tongues of men and of angels, but have not love, I have become a sounding brass or a clanging cymbal. And though I have the gift of prophecy and understand all mysteries and all knowledge, and though I have all faith, so that I could remove mountains, but have not love, I am nothing. And though I bestow all my goods to feed the poor, and though I give my body to be burned, but that not love, it profits me nothing." The very idea here is that it doesn't matter how much you know or how many wonderful things you can do – if you don't love, it's all worthless.

The same can be said for studying the Bible. What is the point of spending time studying the Bible if you are not going to apply it to your life and let it change you and your actions?

Make sure that you are not just puffing yourself up with knowledge but are allowing the word of God to actively transform your heart.

What to Do

- **Pray.** Please don't tell me that you are surprised that this is the first thing that I list. Again, nothing is possible without God. And if you try to make changes in your life without going to God, you will fail. We simply cannot do this life without him. So pray and ask God to change you. Ask God to shine through you, and to transform you into someone who brings glory to him.
- **Make specific goals.** After you have prayed about what you would like to see happen, go ahead and make specific goals. It doesn't have to be anything

major. It could be as simple as setting the goal of having one-on-one time with your kids every week. Or the goal of getting through one day without gossiping. Or the goal of getting rid of the things that you know are going to be a temptation for you. Make small changes and take things one step at a time.
- **Ask for feedback.** Don't be afraid to ask someone that you trust if they can see a change in your behavior, and for them to give you advice on areas that you can work on. Not too long ago the Lord was really showing me that I needed to work on how I talked to and about other people. I can be very sarcastic, and I was finding that my humor had turned into largely just cutting people down. I knew that this was not what the Lord wanted for me, so I asked him to help me change. After a few weeks of making a pointed effort, I asked my husband if he could see a difference. He told me that he could, and now he encourages me in what I am trying to do.

What Not To Do

- **Do not lose focus.** Don't let yourself get sidetracked into making a huge list of rules for yourself and things that you can and cannot do. This is a natural tendency, and one that has been happening for thousands of years. Jesus fought against it with the religious leaders when he was on earth. Remember that the goal of our life is to bring glory and honor to God, and that only he has the power to change hearts. He will show you how he wants you to live and your job is to do it. Not to show how good you are or for your own gain, but to bring glory and honor to him.
- **Do not try to do it on your own.** This goes with my last thought, but again, don't try to do it on your own. The only good that is inside of us is Jesus. So ask

him to transform your life, and then trust him to work in and through you.
- **Do not give up.** You're going to mess up. That's just the way it is. I don't say this to discourage you, but rather to encourage you. When you do mess up, don't give up. Don't throw in the towel and assume that you are never going to change, that God is never going to do anything with you. This couldn't be any further from the truth. 2 Corinthians 12:9 tells us that Jesus says, "My grace is sufficient for you, for my strength is made perfect in weakness." God uses the weak to do great things for his glory.

Chapter 8: Seek Wise Counsel

I want to close out this guide on studying the Bible by encouraging you to seek wise counsel. 1 Peter 5:8 says, "Be sober, be vigilant; because your adversary the devil walks about like a roaring lion, seeking whom he may devour." One of the greatest tools that the enemy uses is to isolate Christians. When we stop seeking wise counsel and start thinking that we can figure out what the Bible is saying without any help, we are opening up ourselves for a world of hurt. As I stated earlier in the guide, our heart is easily deceived, and we can talk ourselves into believing anything. So make sure that you seek wise counsel.

You need to make sure that you have people in your life that can walk with you and help you as you are seeking to study the Bible and walk with God. There are three ways that you can go about seeking wise counsel and fellowship in general. Try to find a church, find a mentor, and find fellowship.

Find a Church

There are people who will argue with me on this fact, but I think that it is absolutely imperative that you should be attending church. Why? For several reasons. Getting together with other believers allows you to find the wise counsel you need. You get the chance to live life alongside other people, and you get the chance to have people pour into your life, and you pour into theirs. Also, the Bible tells us to keep meeting together. Hebrews 10:25 says, "Not forsaking the assembling of ourselves together as is the manner of some, but exhorting one another, and so much the more as you see the day approaching." So if you have a church, don't stop attending. If you don't have a church, then find one.

Step-By-Step Guide to Finding a Church

- Pray. If this guide was a text message, I would insert a smile emoticon here because I know that you are probably getting tired of hearing me say the same thing over and over again. But I can't help it. Prayer is vital. So pray and ask God to direct you to the church that would be the best fit for you.
- Talk to people you know who attend church. A great way to find a church is to simply ask your friend where they go. This depends on your personality though. I know that for me, I want to go and learn about the church before I go with someone else. I don't want to feel pressure to attend somewhere just because my friend goes there. But I am kind of weird like that, so if this matches your personality, then do it. If not, go ahead and skip to step 3.
- Look online for a church. We recently moved to a new area and were looking for a new church. As I stated before I didn't want to ask anyone, so I just looked online at the different churches in the area. I pulled up their websites and looked to see what I could learn about the different churches. What I found was very interesting. It was near Easter time and so all of them had advertisements for what they would be doing for Easter. Some were having famous musicians come in, some had elaborate musicals planned, and several were having Easter egg hunts. Although I knew that my kids would enjoy looking for the eggs, none of those churches jumped out at me. The one that did was one that advertised what the message would be on, and it said that they were going to be taking a close look at who Jesus was by studying his words. This resonated with me, so we went. And we loved it.
- Visit the church. That is the logical next step once you find one that seems appealing. But let me suggest to

you to not make your decision on the first time that you visit. The church that I was telling you about in step 3 was a great church and a perfect fit for our family, but a few Sundays a year they let the children's program take over the entire service. Instead of the usual worship time and Bible lesson, the entire service was filled with cheesy skits and devotional thoughts. My kids loved those Sundays, but they were not exactly my favorite times. I just say this because if you visit a place that has something that doesn't exactly gel one week but you like what you've heard or other things about the church seem to be a good fit, give it another chance. It might just be the place for you.

- Meet with the Pastor. I believe that it is very important to meet with the Pastor before you commit to a church. I learned this the hard way. My husband is a pastor and he had interviewed for a position in a church. We got along with the people that we met, and even though the lead pastor we met was only there to fill in until the church found a new lead; we figured that everything else about the church was a good fit so he agreed to take the position there. A few months into the job the church decided to hire on a new lead pastor. Let's just say that had we met this guy before we accepted the position, we would have never agreed to move there. Within a year my husband was no longer able to serve under the guy's leadership and resigned, and within a year after that the church closed down due to the decisions of that man. So, I tell you this to encourage you to meet with the pastor. Make sure that you get a chance to talk with the man who will be leading and teaching you.
- Commit to a church. Once you have made the choice of what church you are going to attend, commit to being there. Find a way to get involved and serve. The point of the church is to allow you to impact others and others to impact you. This can't happen if you are

just sitting on the sidelines, so make sure to get involved.

Find a Mentor

Proverbs 15:22 states that, "Without counsel, plans go awry, but in the multitude of counselors they are established." It is very important that you find someone that you can go to and talk to about spiritual matters. You need to have someone who can give you wise counsel, instruction, accountability, and support. Basically, a mentor.

At the risk of sounding old-fashioned, I am going to recommend that you find a same-sex mentor. It is okay to have people of the opposite sex whom you look up to and admire in the faith, but when you are seeking out a relationship that will bring with it intense discussions and vulnerability, you need to be wise. There should not be emotional intimacy with someone of the opposite sex who is not your spouse.

There isn't really a formula for finding a mentor. I think that if you try and force a relationship it will not work out very well. But as you get involved in your church, natural relationships will start to form. You will find people who you click with, and you will find someone that you will be able to turn to and who will be able to give you the wise counsel that you need.

Find Fellowship

Acts 2:42 tells us that when the church was first beginning, the believers, "continued steadfastly in the apostles' doctrine and fellowship, in the breaking of bread, and in prayers." We are not created to walk through life alone. We need to be in fellowship with other believers. We need to be living in community. God created us all with different passions and abilities, and his design that we would all fit together and work together to serve and glorify God. You cannot do this without being in fellowship with others.

Ways to Find Fellowship

One time I was talking about this very issue with someone and he told me that he just couldn't find fellowship. He tried, but it was nowhere to be found. Since I know that he does not live on a desert island, I knew that he was just not looking hard enough. Once we talked about some of the options that were available to him, he realized that he did have opportunities and just needed to get out there and do it.

Here are some of the ways that you can find fellowship:

- **Small Group Bible Studies** – Small group Bible studies are important because they allow you to be with a group of believers and dive into the word together. You are able to discuss things with each other and ask questions that you aren't necessarily able to ask in a large church service setting. Fellowship is a natural outpouring of a small group Bible study because you are learning and growing together and sharing your lives.
- **Ministry Groups** – I met my husband while we were serving in ministry together. The very best friends that I have are friends that I made while serving in ministry together. Some of the greatest memories that I have had have come from when I have been serving alongside people in ministry. There is a bond that comes out of ministering alongside someone that doesn't come in any other setting. When

you are united for the same purpose, experiencing the same struggles, and seeing the same results, it has a powerful effect. Find an area in which you would like to minister, and jump in. You will not regret it.

- **Social Activities** – Don't think that finding fellowship has to be all about seriousness. There are several social activities in which you can find fellowship. My husband and I are huge sports fans. We love to play sports, and when we can't play, we love to watch. We have found great times of fellowship with other believers while playing in church softball leagues, watching football, or coaching youth teams together. But don't think that it has to just be sports. I also love music, and I have spent many hours at concerts, dancing and laughing and having fellowship with others. My neck usually hurts the next day from banging my head, but it is definitely worth it.
- **Service Activities** – My favorite church service that I have ever attended was an event called, "Church Outside the Walls." For this event, thirteen of the local churches worked together to perform service projects in the community. While my family and I painted park benches and cleaned up trash, we bonded with our fellow believers in a fun way, and we also witnessed to our community. It was a great experience and I can't wait for the next one.
- **Being Intentional About Reaching Out** - This is a hard one for me to suggest because it's really hard for me to do, but it is an obvious solution. When you make the point to be intentional about reaching out to people and getting to know new people, you will find fellowship. So give it a try. When church is over, don't rush out right away. Stick around for a while and try to meet new people. If you are sitting next to someone you don't know in church, introduce yourself. You'll be amazed at what can happen if you just put yourself out there. I know it's not easy. Believe me. I have more than once used my children as an excuse to not

have to talk to people. But I am going to try to be more intentional about finding fellowship, and I encourage you to do the same.

Now that you have the ways to find wise counsel, do it.

Chapter 9: Conclusion

So there you have it: How to study the Bible. I know that the guide talked about a lot more than just studying the Bible. But it had to. The Word of God is living and active, so the study of the Word of God is living and active.

It has been a great challenge to write this guide, but it has been an incredible blessing as well. I love the fact that I set out to write a guide thinking that I had something to teach, but in reality God used it to show me that I have so much to learn. He showed me that the most important thing to know when studying the Bible is the most important thing to know when doing anything in life: It's all about Jesus. Everything is about him. He draws us to him, he loves us, he saves us, he gives us his word, he transforms our life, and he leads and guides us every day.

I pray that this guide will help you draw closer to God. I pray that you will get a better understanding of his Word. And I pray that you would continue to learn and grow, seeking to know him more every day.

Bibliography

The Woman's Study Bible. Dorothy Kelley Patterson, gen. ed. Nashville: Thomas Nelson, Inc., 1995.

About the Expert

Jane Rodda has been leading Bible Studies for over twenty years, and every time she opens the Word of God she is challenged, encouraged, and grows. Jane loves to learn and loves to teach others the wonderful truths found in the Bible.

Jane wrote "How to Study the Bible for Beginners" to try and help those who are new to studying the Bible learn basic techniques to use to study the Word, and to give suggestions that will help make the Bible come alive.

Jane Rodda knows that she doesn't have it all figured out, and that she never will. But her main goal in life is to encourage others to join her in following Christ and growing in Him.

HowExpert publishes quick 'how to' guides on all topics from A to Z by everyday experts. Visit HowExpert.com to learn more.

Recommended Resources

- HowExpert.com – Quick 'How To' Guides on All Topics from A to Z by Everyday Experts.
- HowExpert.com/free – Free HowExpert Email Newsletter.
- HowExpert.com/books – HowExpert Books
- HowExpert.com/courses – HowExpert Courses
- HowExpert.com/clothing – HowExpert Clothing
- HowExpert.com/membership – HowExpert Membership Site
- HowExpert.com/affiliates – HowExpert Affiliate Program
- HowExpert.com/writers – Write About Your #1 Passion/Knowledge/Expertise & Become a HowExpert Author.
- HowExpert.com/resources – Additional HowExpert Recommended Resources
- YouTube.com/HowExpert – Subscribe to HowExpert YouTube.
- Instagram.com/HowExpert – Follow HowExpert on Instagram.
- Facebook.com/HowExpert – Follow HowExpert on Facebook.

Made in United States
Troutdale, OR
07/02/2023

10939098R00042